**ALSO AVAILABLE FROM MR. MEDIA BOOKS**

**Kicking Through the Ashes** *by Ritch Shydner*

**The Wages of Sin, Vol. IV** *by Keith Brown*

**You'll Need A Guide: Fishing Stories That Aren't Much About the Fish** *by Marshall Craig*

**Will Eisner: A Spirited Life** *(ebook edition) by Bob Andelman*

# Tales From the Trumpster Fire

*A Cartoon Anthology*

## CLAY JONES
### Foreword by Matt Davies

# MR. MEDIA BOOKS
## ST. PETERSBURG, FLORIDA, USA

Visit us on the web!
**ClayToonz.com**
**MrMediaBooks.com**

**Front and back cover design by Clay Jones**
Mr. Media® is a registered trademark of Bob Andelman
MrMedia.com

Cartoons on pages 5, 24, 25, 27, 91, 174, 175, 216, 217, 256 courtesy of CNN

Manufactured in the United States of America
10 9 8 7 6 5 4 3 2 1

ISBN: 978-0-9983937-5-9
Also available as an e-book.

*For Amanda*
*Because yer so bad*

# Contents

# ACKNOWLEDGMENTS

Thank you to Bob Andelman for providing me with this opportunity and getting the project started. Thanks to Hilary Kanter and Laura Moyer, not just for editing this collection but for saving my ass on a daily basis. Thanks to my former bandmate Herman Abinette for software and design advice. I owe a debt to Matt Davies for the foreword, additional words of wisdom on this project, and even naming it. A big thanks to every newspaper and website editor who has ever published my cartoons. Thanks to the crew at CNN Opinion for allowing me to draw for your very serious weekly newsletter and for allowing the inclusion of those cartoons in this very silly book. Thanks to former blog proofreader Frank Foley and current proofer Andréa Denninger. Thanks to The Panolian, the Honolulu Star-Bulletin, The Free Lance-Star, and Creators Syndicate. My son, Clayton Michael, deserves a shout-out as well as Dr. Christopher Fink, Gordon Johnson, Bobby Hebert, JP Trostle, Walt Handelsman, Ann Telnaes, Mike Peters, Rosie O'Donnell, Dallas Ryan, Karen Black, the Howell family and Kelly Green. To my two brothers, Jimmy and Bobby, for their support and my niece, Rene Holt, for being a voice of reason in a hostile atmosphere.

Amanda, thank you for being much smarter than me and for not killing me in my sleep after all the times I've called you back to fix something in Word. It will happen again.

Finally, to everyone who has read, laughed or cursed at, clicked like, shared, or commented on a cartoon, or bought a shirt, mug, or this book…THANK YOU. This is your book. I love each and every single one of you. You rock!

# FOREWORD
## By Matt Davies

I admit I am biased. We political cartoonists can be difficult to please - ornery and hyper-critical of one another at times. But for some reason Clay Jones has mostly said pleasant things about my own cartoons, so he holds an exceptionally warm place in my heart. Clay and I are roughly the same age. In the early 1990s when we were in our 20s, we simultaneously struggled to gain attention, eagerly occupying that exciting, outcast space reserved for unknown cartoonists.

I remember the first time I saw a Clay Jones cartoon, a reprint in USA Today. The drawing was scribbly and didn't register heavily on the MacNelly art scale that so many cartoonists of the period adhered to. It was searingly funny and clever. We sought each other out at a subsequent cartoonist gathering and enthusiastically stayed up too late playing pool, drinking beer and talking shit (which is what cartoonists are best at).

While Clay was always a clever, funny cartoonist, in the past few years something clicked under the combination of his leaving The Free Lance-Star in Fredericksburg, Virginia, and the installation of Donald J. Trump in the Oval Office, which unleashed in Jones a raging derecho. Late at night, while other cartoonists are merely sleeping, Clay has downed what I imagine must be his seventh cup of coffee and drawn three cartoons mocking the news cycle's last few hours of outrage. His depiction of President Donald Trump includes a yellow lightning bolt-esque bouffant which serves as a resplendent avatar for the energy Clay infuses into his work. Across the political spectrum, editorial cartoonists employ signature approaches to skewering. Some make their political incisions with scalpel-like precision, others with a nail-encrusted 2x4. I would place Clay's cartoons in the "boat-horn-at-Sunday-morning-Mass" category.

Clay, a Renaissance man, is also known in cartooning circles for his musical abilities. He fronted a grunge band called Corporate T-shirt, a CD of which I still own! He likens his musical abilities to his cartooning style and self describes as a "sloppy guitar player and sloppy cartoonist." He shortchanges himself on both counts. His cartoon writing is thoughtful, energetic, chuckle-inducing and invariably cleverly executed.

After thumbing through the fiery collection of material that these words precede, I'm sure you'll agree with me.

When pressed for this foreword as to the qualities he brings to the art form, "I think you gotta be a little messed up to write good political cartoons," he responded.

A compelling invitation to read on…

*Matt Davies is a Pulitzer Prize-winning cartoonist with two Herblock Awards for Newsday.*

Courtesy of CNN

# Introduction
## By Clay Jones

Every political cartoonist has days where it's difficult to write an idea. What's worse than that are slow news days where we can't find a subject. I haven't had a day like that since June 16, 2015. On that day, Donald J. Trump came down the golden escalator and before a crowd he paid to be there, railed about Mexicans and announced his candidacy for president.

Readers tell me all the time how great Donald Trump is for me as a political cartoonist. Why, the ideas must just write themselves. Trump has not been as good for cartoonists as you might think. Whereas before there were days I couldn't find a subject, now I often want Trump to shut up long enough so I can cover his last racist comment or outrage. Another problem is, it's hard to satirize satire. Today, headlines in The New York Times and The Washington Post look like they were written for The Onion.

On the business side of it, he's terrible. I have lost clients because I won't stop drawing Donald Trump. I've had potential clients tell me they can't run anything, pro or con, on him. And then there are the editors who actually like Trump, and they respond to my unwanted solicitation like trolls on Facebook. Have you ever had a newspaper editor call you "snowflake"? I have.

On top of all that, I had to create a cartoon of a cartoon. It's extremely hard to make a caricature of Donald Trump more ridiculous than the actual Donald Trump. The hair, the lips, the eyebrows, the fake tan and the ridiculously long tie (which I was the first cartoonist in the nation to draw). You might say it doesn't look like Trump, but you know it's Donald Trump. Liberals tell me it's their favorite caricature of him. Members of the Trump cult are enraged by it, but they know it's Donald Trump. It may not actually look like him physically, but I think it nails his personality. Ugly, stupid and orange.

But Donald Trump is good for political cartoonists in a lot of ways. A long time ago, someone made the observation that when times are good for political cartoonists and comedians, it's bad for America. Right now, it is really good for political cartoonists. Sorry, America.

I hear from readers that my cartoons are helping them get through this disaster. I'm always overwhelmed to learn I'm someone's form of therapy. When Trump announced his candidacy, we laughed at him. Now the world is laughing at us. With this book, I hope you can laugh at us too.

Laughing at Donald Trump is better than being afraid of him, because that's what they want. They want us to be afraid. Knowing that you, dear reader, are laughing at my cartoons is therapy for me.

When I was brand new at this and attending my first cartoonists convention in 1991, a grizzled old cartooning veteran drew a caricature of Richard Nixon in an autograph book I was passing around. He wrote, "You'll never see the likes of me again." It was at least 15 years after Watergate and he still wasn't over Nixon. And he was wrong.

As you go through this book 20 years from now, I hope you're over Trump. I hope we all are. And I hope we never see the likes of him again. And as you go through this book years from now, don't forget this really happened. And if you're reading this and you weren't alive yet, YES! This shit really happened.

I couldn't have made all this up by myself.

JONES
CLAYTOONZ.COM

Election night 2016.

# Chapter One

# Impeach

Even on the campaign trail, Trump made promises that would violate the Constitution and a president's oath of office. Each day in office, he gave reasons he should be impeached. Finally, in October 2019, he gave Americans a reason to impeach they can't ignore.

September 2019

September 2018

April 2018

September 2018

September 2019

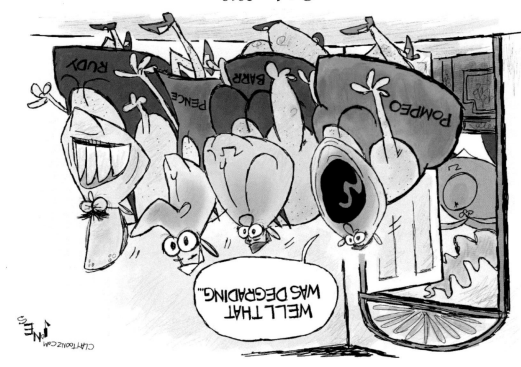

October 2019

September 2019

October 2019

October 2019

October 2019

October 2019

October 2019

October 2019

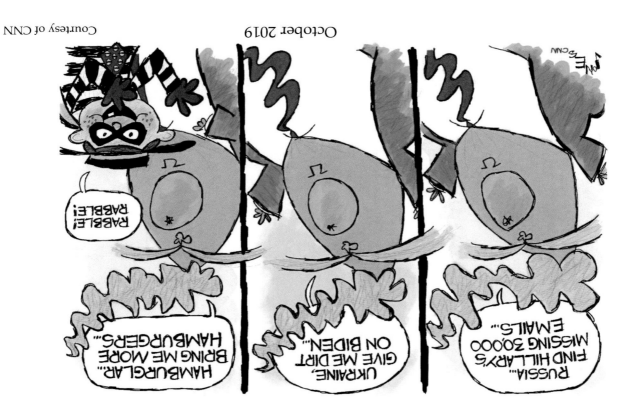

October 2019

October 2019

October 2019

October 2019

Courtesy of CNN

October 2019

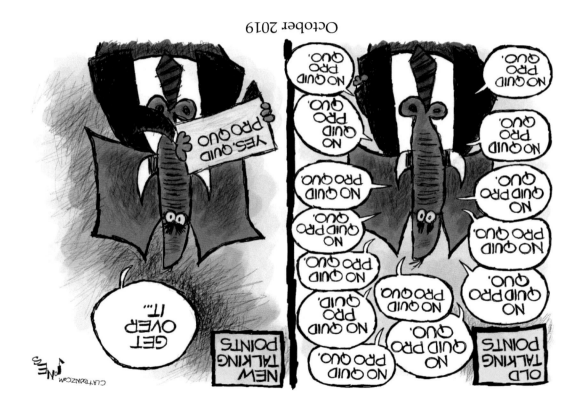

# Chapter Two

# A Narcissistic, Racist Idiot Runs for President

Is America really mean, cruel, racist and stupid enough to put a mean, cruel, racist, stupid, narcissistic reality TV show host and con man into the White House?

P.S. This is where you get to see the earliest versions of my Trump caricature.

February 2016

February 2016

March 2016

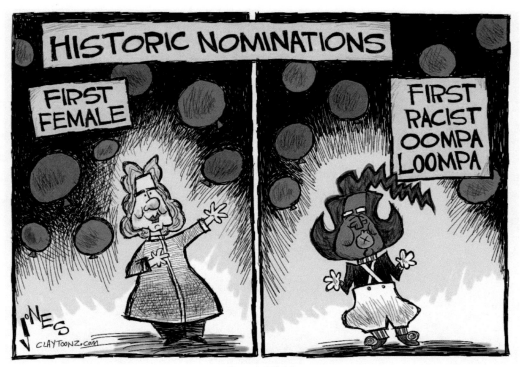

June 2016

June 2016

June 2016

July 2015

July 2016

July 2015

August 2015

August 2015

CLAYTOONZ.COM

September 2015

September 2015

November 2015

December 2015

July 2016

August 2016

September 2016. A reader alerted me that she found
this cartoon on a coffee mug in Wisconsin.

October 2016

CLAYTOONZ.COM
JoNES

October 2016

October 2016

November 2016. This was drawn the day after the election. Remember when we thought we could get back to normal and start liking each other again?

November 2016. From my live blog on election night. This is the best cartoon that came out of it, and the Ottawa Citizen published it. (If you're a Republican, Ottawa is in Canada.)

November 2016. A couple of days after the election. I was still in recovery.

# Chapter Three:

# Putin's Puppet

Did Vladimir Putin and Russia help Donald Trump win the presidency? Yes.

December 2016

January 2017

January 2017

April 2017

September 2017

September 2017

October 2017

November 2017

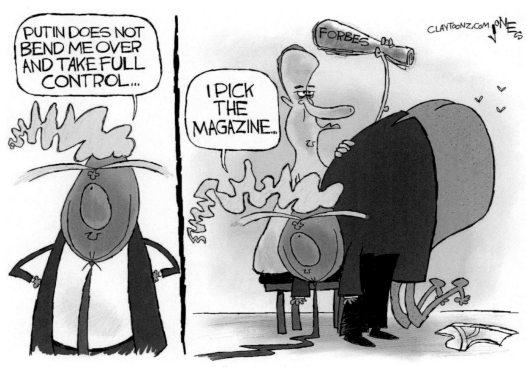

January 2018

September 2018

April 2019

September 2019

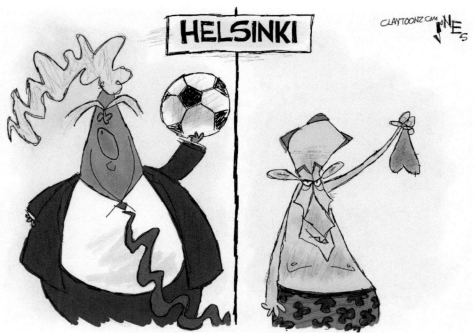

July 2018. I apologize for this cartoon.
This has gotta be the worst Putin caricature I've ever drawn.

# Chapter Four

# Liar in Chief

As this book was published, Donald Trump had told over 13,000 lies.

CLAYTOONZ.COM JONES

January 2017

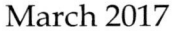

March 2017

June 2017

November 2018

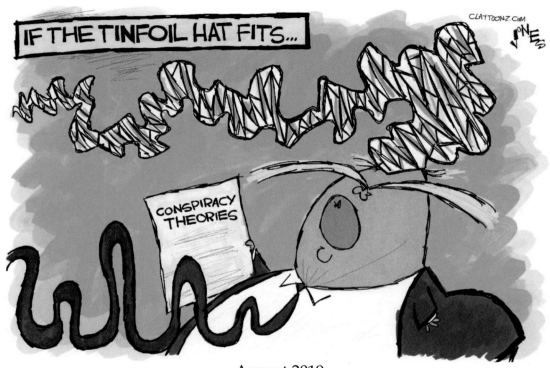

August 2019

August 2019

OVERCOMING A BRUTAL WINTER OF PHONY WITCH HUNTS AND BONE SPURS... GENERAL WASHINGTON RAMMED THE SOROS-FUNDED RAMPARTS AND SAVED THE AIRPORTS FROM CARAVAN INVASIONS..."WHERE FINALLY..."HE LOCKED HER UP..."REMEMBER THE à LA MODE!..."

PREZ

TANKS FOR THE HISTORY LESSON

CLAYTOONZ.COM

jONES

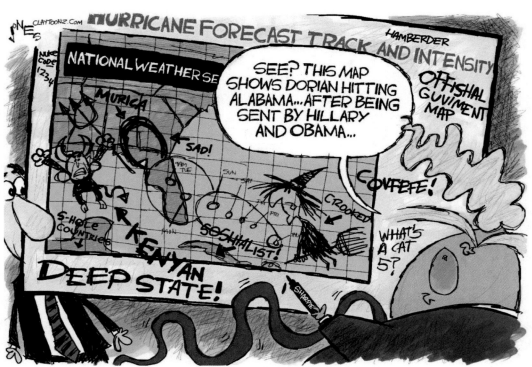

September 2019

April 2019

# Chapter Five

# Fun With Corruption

The entire Trump administration is corrupt.

November 2016

October 2017

December 2017

December 2017

March 2018

April 2018

October 2018

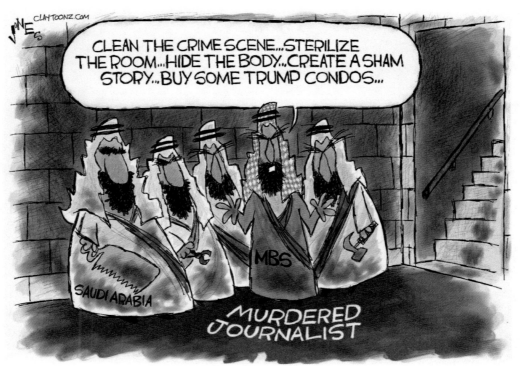

October 2018

December 2018

January 2019

April 2019

September 2019

September 2019

October 2019

# Chapter Six

# Immigration and a Racist Vanity Project

In case you're a Republican, Mexico still hasn't paid for it.

January 2017. Donald Trump is a racist.

April 2017. Donald Trump is a racist jerk.

June 2018. The Orlando Weekly (in case you're a Republican, that's in Orlando) used this cartoon for their cover.

July 2018

July 2018

July 2018

August 2018

September 2017. A hurricane hit Texas right when America had a racist president.

January 2019. America had a new speaker of the House,
and Donald Trump went for a photo-op.

February 2019

May 2019

June 2019

WELCOME TO
DONALD
TRUMP'S
AMERICA

July 2019

August 2019

November 2018

# Chapter Seven

# Fake News and Alternative Facts

Facts have a liberal bias, and Donald Trump hates a free press.

January 2017

January 2018

May 2018

May 2018

August 2018

"...FOR CNN FROM THE TRUMP RALLY...," I'M JIM ACOSTA..."

August 2018. Donald Trump once said the National Enquirer should have a Pulitzer Prize.

September 2018. Bob Woodward gave me a copy of his book "Fear" for a signed print of this cartoon.

# Chapter Eight

# Trust Fund Babies

Corrupt, stupid, racist apples don't fall far from corrupt, stupid, racist trees.

December 2016

September 2016. Idiot hateful son number one, Don Jr., tweeted a comparison of bad Skittles to Syrian refugees. Seriously. Oh, and Trump had a CRAZY doctor.

May 2017

July 2017. Junior invited Russians into Trump's campaign headquarters.

July 2017

July 2017

August 2017. By the time General Kelly left the White House, his credibility was on par with Ivanka's.

January 2018

May 2019

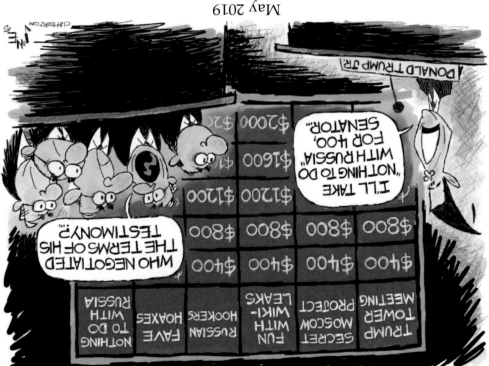

June 2019

July 2019

July 2019

July 2019

September 2019

# Chapter Nine

# Friends and Sycophants

Donald Trump has friends in low and deplorable places.

November 2016

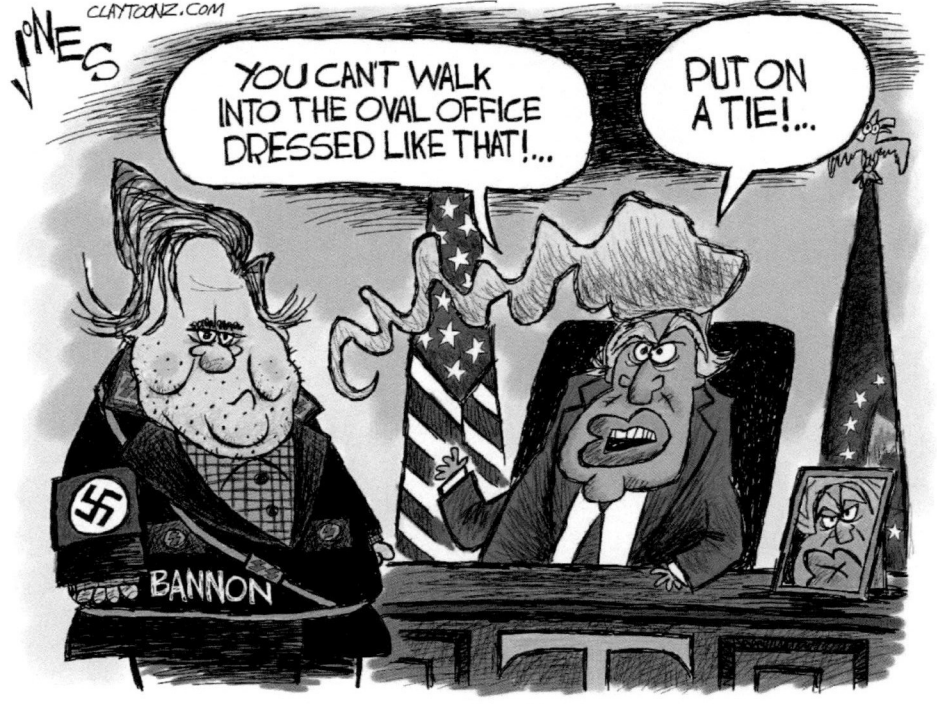

November 2016

November 2016. Mike Pence went to Broadway and hated it.

February 2017. Betsy DeVos wants guns in schools for protection from bears. Seriously.

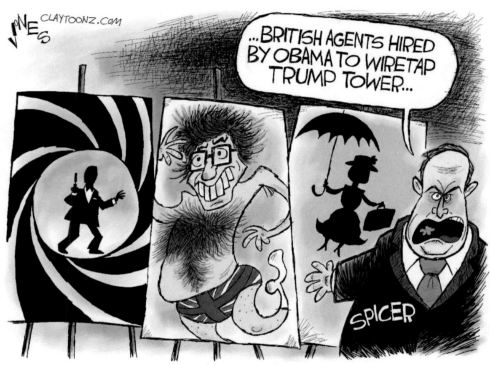

March 2017

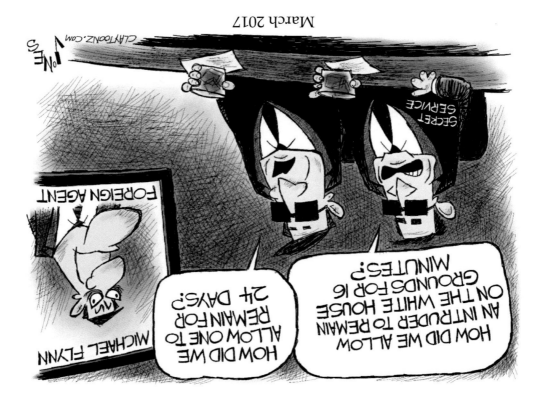

March 2017

April 2017

May 2017

June 2017

November 2016

August 2017

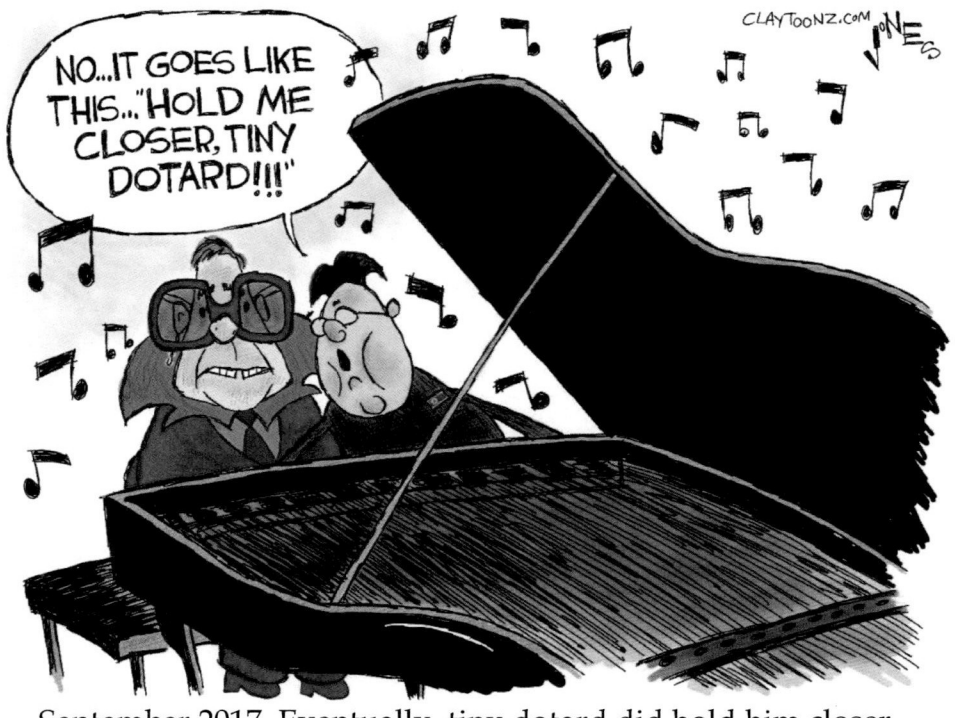

September 2017. Eventually, tiny dotard did hold him closer.

October 2017

November 2018

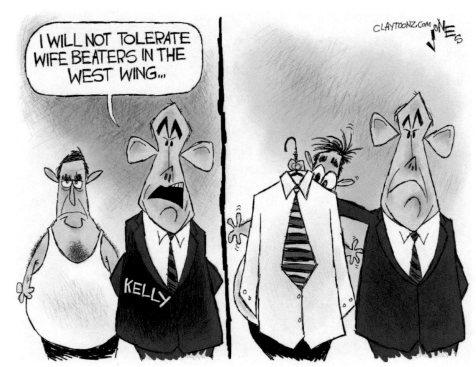

February 2018

March 2018

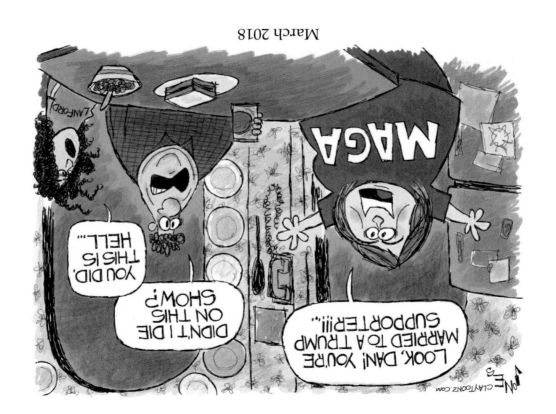

May 2018

May 2018

June 2018

June 2018.

July 2018

July 2018

August 2018

August 2018

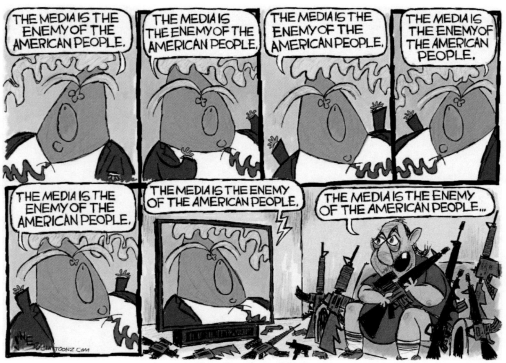

September 2018

September 2018. Plaid Shirt Guy's mother requested a copy of this cartoon.

October 2018

October 2018

December 2018

January 2019

January 2019

March 2019. I asked George if he'd give a quote for this book. He didn't call me back.

May 2019

May 2019

July 2019

July 2019

July 2019

August 2019

August 2019

August 2019. This is a play on a cartoon that ran in The International New York Times that killed all cartoons in The New York Times.

September 2019. I'm still surprised I got away with this one.

Courtesy of CNN

June 2019. Jay Sekulow, William Barr and Rudy Giuliani all have little dinghies.

IN CASE OF CHAOS
BREAK GLASS

September 2019

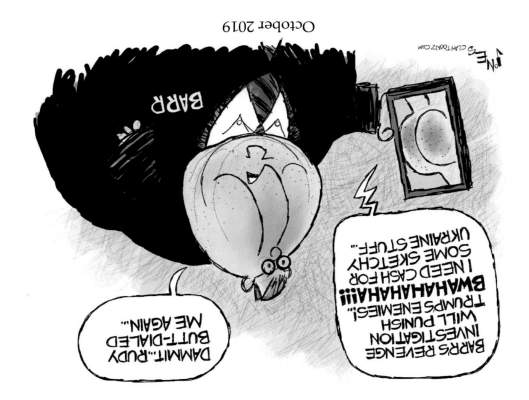

October 2019

# Chapter Ten

# Fun With Racism

Donald Trump is a racist.

December 2016

May 2016

June 2016

July 2016. Trump retweeted a Jewish star in a picture with money.

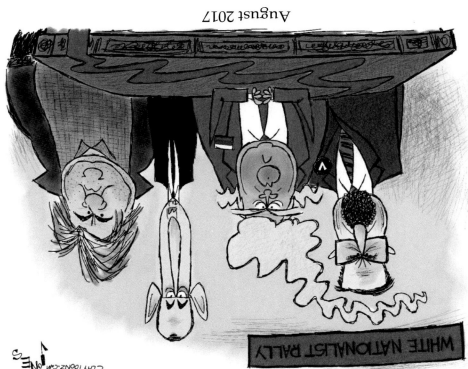

August 2017

WHITE NATIONALIST RALLY

CLAYTOONZ.COM

September 2016. During the campaign, Trump called for deportations of people of a specific religion.

November 2016

August 2017. Charlottesville.

Septtember 2017

October 2017. Puerto Rico.

October 2017

December 2017

January 2018

September 2018. I know a Gary who will tell you he's the least racist person you know.

October 2018

February 2019. Racist Republicans will save us from anti-semitism.

February 2019

March 2019

April 2019

May 2019. I like to call Steve Mnuchin "Baby Fishmouth."

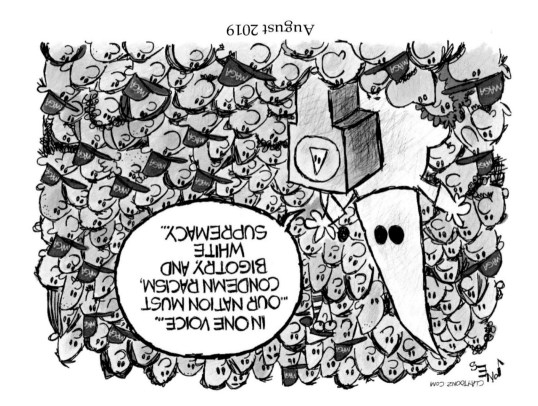

August 2019

August 2019

August 2019

September 2019. From when he talked about nuking hurricanes.

# Chapter Eleven

# Narcissistic Trump Baby

Stable genius. Best brain. Chosen one. Your favorite president.
Despite his ego, Donald Trump is an insecure little baby because deep down inside, he knows no one will ever truly love him.

December 2016. This cartoon actually won an award
from the government of Iran. I turned it down.

June 2017

July 2017

January 2018

February 2018

February 2018

May 2018

July 2018

July 2018

November 2018

March 2019. A Trump Sharpie cartoon before Sharpiegate.

August 2019

August 2019

Courtesy of CNN

August 2019

# Chapter Twelve

# Fun With Sexism

Donald Trump is a misogynistic, sexist pig.

September 2016

October 2016

November 2017

December 2017

August 2018. Aretha Franklin, 1942 – 2018

October 2018

April 2019

May 2019. Alabama outlawed ALL abortions. Friends of Trump.

September 2018

# Chapter Thirteen

# An International Embarrassment

The world is literally laughing at us.

April 2017

May 2017

PARIS CLIMATE PULLOUT

June 2017

April 2018

July 2018. Trump doesn't want to complicate our relationship
with Russia after they attacked us.

September 2018

May 2019

NO! WE WOULDN'T BE INTERESTED IN A BLOODY TRADE!...

May 2019. A year into Trump's trade war and they still support him.

May 2019

July 2019

August 2019

"SORRY GREENLAND DIDN'T WORK OUT... BUT I GOTS ANOTHER DEAL THAT SHOULD TICKLE YOUR FANCY..."

October 2019

October 2019

# Chapter Fourteen

# Trump Fuckery

An assortment of Trump disaster after Trump disaster.

May 2017

May 2017

July 2017

August 2017. This is one of my all-time favorites.

September 2017

"GRAB THEM BY THE..."

"SOME VERY FINE PEOPLE"

"I LIKE PEOPLE WHO WEREN'T CAPTURED"

"FIRE THAT SON OF A..."

October 2017

February 2018

March 2018

January 2019

January 2019. Someone projected this cartoon onto the
side of a federal building in San Francisco.

April 2019

June 2019

March 2010

March 2018

June 2019. See you in 2020.

# About Clay Jones

Clay Jones is a self-syndicated political cartoonist whose work is distributed to newspapers and news sites across the United States and around the world. He also draws a weekly cartoon for CNN Opinion's weekly newsletter, Provoke/Persuade. Clay was represented by Creators Syndicate (2000-13) until he left to start his own syndicate. His career began in 1990 at The Panolian, a weekly newspaper in Batesville, Mississippi. Clay also worked for the Daily Leader in Brookhaven, Mississippi, the Honolulu Star-Bulletin, and The Free Lance-Star in Fredericksburg, Virginia. He previously worked as a freelance cartoonist for The Daily Dot, The Seattle Times and The Costa Rica Star.

Clay won "Best Cartoon" in the National Newspaper Association's Better Newspaper Contest (2018), as well as several state awards in Mississippi, Hawaii and Virginia. Additionally, he was the finalist for the Herblock Award (2019), and rejected a weird "free speech" award from the government of Iran.

A collection of his work is archived at the Mattie Sink Memorial Library at Mississippi State University. An early collection of his cartoons, titled "Knee-Deep in Mississippi," was distributed by Pelican Publishing (1997). And his work was displayed in an exhibit at the Jewish Museum Berlin (2017).

His daily cartoons are featured in about 50 newspapers and have been reprinted in The New York Times, The Washington Post, the Los Angeles Times, USA Today, The Chicago Tribune, the Chicago Sun-Times, the St. Louis Post-Dispatch, The Dallas Morning News, the Winnipeg Free Press, the Ottawa Citizen, the Daily Beast, BuzzFeed, Newsweek and Time Magazine. They've been seen on CNN, MSNBC and CSPAN.

Clay plays and writes 90s-style alt-rock on guitar. He released the album "No Thanks To Hancock" with the band Corporate T-Shirt.

He lives somewhere in the Washington, D.C, suburbs of Northern Virginia.

**Follow Clay**
Website: claytoonz.com
Facebook: facebook.com/clayjones
Twitter:  @claytoonz
Instagram: @clayjonz
**Watch Clay Draw**
YouTube: youtube.com/c/Claytoonzcom
**Buy Claytoonz merch at**
teespring.com/stores/clay-toonz-merchandise

**Also available from Mr. Media Books**

MrMediaBooks.com

**Also available from Mr. Media Books**
MrMediaBooks.com

4585124R00162

Made in the USA
Coppell, TX
18 December 2020